BRUTAL IMAGINATION

A MARIAN WOOD BOOK

PUBLISHED BY G. P. PUTNAM'S SONS

A MEMBER OF PENGUIN PUTNAM INC.

NEW YORK

CORNELIUS EADY

BRUTAL IMAGINATION

p | *o* | *e* | *m* | *s*

A MARIAN WOOD BOOK
Published by G. P. Putnam's Sons
Publishers Since 1838
a member of
Penguin Putnam Inc.
375 Hudson Street
New York, NY 10014

Library of Congress Cataloging-in-Publication Data

Eady, Cornelius, date.
   Brutal imagination : poems / Cornelius Eady.
      p.   cm.
   "A Marian Wood book."
   ISBN 0-399-14718-7 (hardback edition)
      1. Afro-Americans—Poetry.   2. Race awareness—Poetry.
3. Race relations—Poetry.   I. Title.

PS3555.A35 B78   2001   00-062674
811'.54—dc21
   ISBN 0-399-14720-9 (paperback edition)

Printed in the United States of America

10   9   8   7   6   5   4   3   2   1

This book is printed on acid-free paper ∞

Book design by Judith Stagnitto Abbate / Abbate Design

ACKNOWLEDGMENTS

Some of the poems in this collection have appeared in the following:

Ploughshares: How I Got Born, My Heart, Who Am I?, Sightings.

Fourteen Hills: Running Man, Miss Look's Dream (Under the title "The Younger Sister's Dream").

"My Face" first appeared in the anthology *In Defense of Mumia* (Writers and Readers Publishing, Inc., 1996), S. E. Anderson and Tony Medina, eds.

Many of the poems in the *Running Man* section were used as the basis of the text for the jazz-opera *Running Man* (© 1999, Murray/ Eady), that ran from February 16 to March 14, 1999, at the HERE Performing Arts Space in New York City (story and music by Diedre Murray; text by Cornelius Eady; directed by Diane Paulus; produced by Music-Theatre Group; Lyn Austin, producing director; Diane Wondisford, general director). My thanks to all involved with the production, including the fine cast and musicians, and most especially to Diedre and to Diane Paulus.

The quote from Jean Valentine is used with permission of the author, and is from her book *The Cradle of the Real Life* (Wesleyan University Press, 2000).

Thanks to my friend Chuck Wachtel for providing the spark.

Finally, my thanks and love always to my first reader, Sarah Micklem, and to my editor, Marian Wood, the fiercest friend a book ever had.

To Toi, Sarah, Carolyn,

and

the Cave Canem family

Then they let him go. Not

wanting him alive, not wanting him dead.

Their knees grind over the sea

and make malice. What is love? What does love do?

—JEAN VALENTINE, "BLACK FOR THE PEOPLE"

CONTENTS

BRUTAL IMAGINATION:

The speaker is the young black man
Susan Smith claimed
kidnapped her children.

HOW I GOT BORN

Though it's common belief
That Susan Smith willed me alive
At the moment
Her babies sank into the lake

When called, I come.
My job is to get things done.
I am piecemeal.
I make my living by taking things.

So now a mother needs me clothed
In hand-me-downs
And a knit cap.

Whatever.
We arrive, bereaved
On a stranger's step.
Baby, they weep,
Poor child.

MY HEART

Susan Smith has invented me because
Nobody else in town will do what
She needs me to do.
I mean: jump in an idling car
And drive off with two sad and
Frightened kids in the back.
Like a bad lover, she has given me a poisoned heart.
It pounds both our ribs, black, angry, nothing but business.
Since her fear is my blood
And her need part mythical,
Everything she says about me is true.

WHO AM I?

Who are you, mister?
One of the boys asks
From the eternal backseat
And here is the one good thing:
If I am alive, then so, briefly, are they,
Two boys returned, three and one,
Quiet and scared, bunched together
Breathing like small beasts.
They can't place me, yet there's
Something familiar.
Though my skin and sex are different, maybe
It's the way I drive
Or occasionally glance back
With concern,
Maybe it's the mixed blessing
Someone, perhaps circumstance,
Has given us,
The secret thrill of hiding,
Childish, in plain sight,
Seen, but not seen,
As if suddenly given the power
To move through walls,
To know every secret without permission.
We roll sleepless through the dark streets, but inside
The cab is lit with brutal imagination.

SIGHTINGS

A few nights ago
A man swears he saw me pump gas
With the children
At a convenience store
Like a punchline you get the next day,
Or a kiss in a dream that returns while
You're in the middle of doing
Something else.

I left money in his hand.

Mr. _____ who lives in _____,
South Carolina,
Of average height
And a certain weight
Who may or may not
Believe in any of the
Basic recognized religions,
Saw me move like an angel
In my dusky skin
And knit hat.

Perhaps I looked him in the eye.

Ms. _____ saw a glint of us
On which highway?
On the street that's close
To what landmark?

She now recalls
The two children in the back
Appeared to be behaving.

Mr. _____ now knows he heard
The tires of the car
Everyone is looking for
Crunch the gravel
As I pulled up,
In the wee, wee hours
At the motel where
He works the night desk.

I signed or didn't sign the register.
I took or didn't take the key from his hand.
He looked or forgot to look
As I pulled off to park in front
Of one of the rooms at the back.

Did I say I was traveling with kids?
Who slept that night
In the untouched beds?

MY FACE

If you are caught
In my part of town
After dark,
You are not lost;
You are abandoned.

All that the neighbors will tell
Your kin
Is that you should
Have known better.

All they will do
Is nod their heads.
They will feel sorry
For you,

But rules are rules,
And when you were
Of a certain age
Someone pointed
A finger
In the wrong direction

And said:
All they do
Is fuck and drink
All they're good for
Ain't worth a shit.

You recall me now
To the police artist.
It wasn't really my face
That stared back that day,
But it was that look.

SUSAN SMITH'S POLICE REPORT

My shape came from out-of-nowhere.
The way some things don't belong
That's the way

I clanged up to the car
Trapped by a badly timed light.
Her poor kids never saw our image

Swell in the rearview mirror.
I was the danger of bulk; fast,
Nervous fingers

Barked the unlocked door open
And in I flooded, all the heartache
A lonely stretch of road can give.

Then she was alone, blinking in
The sight of an indifferent moon
Above the pines.

This, she swore, was the sound
Of my voice.

WHERE AM I?

Looking for Michael and Alex means
That the bushes have not whispered,
That the trees hold only shade
That the lake still insists on being a lake.

I flicker from TV to TV. My flier sits
On their grandmother's easy chair. I hover
Over so many lawns, so many cups of coffee.

I pour from lip to lip. The town blossoms
In yellow ribbons, sprinkled like bread crumbs
Or bait. I crackle from cell phones and shortwave,

I am listened for in alleys. Looking for Michael
And Alex means each car is scanned at the
Drive-thru windows, that sightings are hoped for

At the self-serve pumps. Clerks long for the crook
Of my arm, reaching for diapers and snacks.
So many days I have loped from ear to ear,

From beauty parlor to church. They count the days
Till someone comes back. We've never left.

THE LAKE

When called, I come.
My job
Is to get things
Done.

Our hands grip the wheel
As I steer toward
The lake.

The children and I
Have been driving
For days.

Ever look someone
You know
Straight in the eye

And have them look
Right through you? That's been
Our fugitive lives.

They think:
They'll have to sleep
Sometime,
But we don't do things
The way you do.

They think:
Sooner or later
They'll have
To eat,

But a deal's a deal.
Our appetite behaves.
Our day seeps
Through yours.

Ever try to say
Something,
And know what you said
Slid past an ear?

That's the way these headlights
Rake the road along the lake.
That's the way
Her children yawn in the
Back seat.

THE LAW

I'm a black man, which means,
In Susan's case,
That I pour out of a shadow
At a traffic light,

But I'm also a mother,
Which is why she has me promise,
"I won't hurt your kids,"
Before I drift down the road.

I'm a mother,
Which is why we sing
Have mercy, come home,
No questions asked.

But I'm black, and we both know
The law.
Who's going to believe
That we had no choice
But to open that door?

Who's going to care
That it was now or
Never,
That there was no time
To unbuckle them,

That it was take the car
Or leave the car?

I'm black, which means
I mustn't slow down.
I float in forces
I can't always control,

But I'm also a mother,
Which is why
I hope
I'm as good as my word.

She knew she could get further with this
if she said a black man did it.
—*A black resident of Union, South Carolina*

WHY I AM NOT A WOMAN

How far do you think we'd have gotten
If I'd jumped in her car, a car I wanted
For who knows what,
A woman,
And not noticed the paraphernalia?
The rattles, the child's seat?
Had smelled the spills, the dried pee,
The cloudy musk of old formula?

Even if I had pushed her out, head wild
With all I guessed I'd taken,
How many minutes,
After my foot brushed a ball,
After my eyes cooled down and focused on
The rubble of play,

How many lights do you think I'd run
Before all the stuff they'd dropped
Over the years
Into the small cracks; the straws, the cold
Fries, the pacifier,

How long do you think the cops would listen
Had Susan not sworn
I was black, I was a bad dream,
The children didn't mean a thing
To that woman.

ONE TRUE THING

I was made to be a driver, but the truth is, I was, from the
Beginning, Susan's admiral. The sheriff suspects
I sped the car into the lake like the christening of a great
Ship. The fact is, momentum has more than one cure.
You should think of a rowboat, a prank of tiny holes drilled
Into the bottom. A fast car hits the water like a wall of brick
And glue. But a car, gently pushed, quieter than a cop's
Imagination, will bob out, fill up, then roll like a leaky can.

COMPOSITE

I am not the hero of this piece.
I am only a stray thought, a solution.
But now my face is stuck to lampposts, glued
To plate glass, my forehead gets stapled
To my hat.

I am here, and here I am not.
I am a door that opens, and out walks
No-one-can-help-you.
Now I gaze, straight into your eye,
From bulletin boards, tree trunks.

I am papered everywhere,
A blizzard called
You see what happens?
I turn up when least expected.
If you decide to buy some milk,

If you decide to wash your car,
If you decide to mail a letter,

I might tumbleweed onto a pant leg.
You can stare, and stare, but I can't be found.
Susan has loosed me on the neighbors,
A cold representative,
The scariest face you could think of.

*In 1989, in Boston, Charles Stuart
killed his pregnant wife and
shot himself in a scheme
to collect insurance money.
He told the police the assailant
was a young black male.*

CHARLES STUART IN THE HOSPITAL

Susan Smith now knows what
Charles Stuart knew in Boston:
We do quick, but sloppy work.
All these details:

How tall was I? the police asked Charles,
And ask Susan,
But I vary; I seem smaller and taller
After dusk.
What was the tone of my voice?
Did I growl like a hound as I waved
The pistol in their face?
Was I as desperate as a teenaged boy,
Horny for a sweetheart's kiss?

Here's what I told Susan:
"I won't harm your kids."
But if the moment was mine,
Why would I say that?

I sit with her at the station
The way I sat with Charles
At the hospital:
A shadow on the water glass,
Changing hues,

The slant of my nose and eyes.
Depending on the light
And the question.

Charles rocks in bed with the bullet
We gave ourselves.
How far away was I? We never stopped
To think.
We were in a hurry.
In Boston and South Carolina
I was hungry for a car
And didn't much care how I got it.
Deadly impatient, Charles tells the cops,
But if I couldn't be seen,
But why would I do it that way?
Why do wives and children seem to attract me?

I sat with Charles the way I sit
With Susan; like anyone, and no one,
Changing clothes,
Putting on and taking off ski caps,
Curling and relaxing my hair,
Trying hard to become sense.

UNCLE TOM IN HEAVEN

My name is mud; let's get that out
Of the way first. I am not a child.
I was made to believe that God
Kept notes, ran a tab on the blows,
So many on one cheek, so many on
The other.

I watch another black man pour from a
White woman's head. I fear
He'll live the way I did, a brute,
A flimsy ghost of an idea. Both
Of us groomed to go only so far.

That was my duty. I'm well aware
Of what I've become; a name
Children use to separate themselves
On a playground. It doesn't matter
To know I'm someone else's lie,

Anything human can slip, and that's enough
To make grown men worry about
Their accent, where their ambition might
Stray. It doesn't help anything to tell you
I was built to be a hammer,
A war cry. Like him, nobody knew me,

But in my prime, I filled the streets, worried
Into the eardrum, scared up thoughts
Of laws and guns. How I would love
Not to be dubious,

But I am a question whole races spend
Their time trying to answer. My author
Believed in God, and being denied the
Power to hate her,

I watch another black man roam the land,
Dull in his invented hide.

UNCLE BEN WATCHES THE LOCAL NEWS

Like him, I live, but never agreed to it.
A hand drew me out of some mad concern.
I was pulled together
To give, to cook
But never eat.

So I know this fellow, this guy
They're overturning the world
To find. He and I were
Stamped from the same ink.
I look at them look, high, low,
Over, under. I know
What that white lady thinks,

She's as sad and crazy as the smile
They've quilled under my nose.

JEMIMA'S DO-RAG

I crown her secret, the hair
The world seems to dread.
At night, alone, after work has loosened
Its grip, and the muscles of her smile
Can relax, at the dresser, beside the
Washbasin, down comes the beauty
They try so hard to bind.

I hear there's a man on the street,
Eyes dead as marbles, dodging
The law. They say his cap is made
Of wool. If he sleeps, I bet he dreams
Like we do, scalp uncoiled, nobody's helper,
No one's aunt.

BUCKWHEAT'S LAMENT

My family tells me this white gang I run with will
Grow up, and leave me behind. Our bones
Will change, and so will their affection. I will
Be a childlike man who lives in a shack. Just
Wait, they promise, my hair will become
Hoo-doo. The white girls will deny how we rassled,
What we saw. They laugh

Wait 'til you're *grown*. And I hear this sad place
At the middle of that word where they live,
Where they wait for my skin to go sour.

STEPIN FETCHIT READS THE PAPER

Not the dead actor,
Historically speaking, but the ghost
Of the scripts, the bumbling fake
Of an acrobat, the low-pitched anger
Someone mistook for stupid.

This so-called bruiser rattling the streets,
Heavy with children, I'd like to
Tell him what a thankless job
It is to go along to get along.
All the nuances can and will
Be rubbed smooth and by the time
It's over,

By the time you're dead and the people
You thought you were doing this
On behalf of are long forgotten,

There's only an image left that they
Name you after, toothy, slow,
Worthy of a quick kick in the pants.
I used to have bones, I'd tell him.
It was a story that
Rubbed out my human walk.

THE UNSIGNED CONFESSION OF MR. ZERO

No car, no road, no tires, no hands, no fingers, no feet,
No gas pedal, no turn signals, no stoplights, no watch cap,
No legs, no pants, no worn shirt, no blank eyes,
No heavy lids, no cold voice, no threat, no dark skin,

No lying in wait, no click of a handle, no mother's scream,
No silence at her questions, no height, no weight,
No strange needs, no sense of adventure, no breath,
No nappy hair, no memories, no one to impress,

No hunger, no shit, no piss, no weariness, no reaction,
No family, no ideas, no history, no favorite song,
No blood pressure, no guilt, no sleep or dreams,
No steering wheel, no rearview mirror, no ID.

Somewhere near the bushes. On the periphery.
A noise you can't easily locate. I am the heaviness
The sheriff thinks he detects on Susan Smith's tongue,
The story she tries to hold between her teeth and gums.

WHAT I'M MADE OF

Susan fills our hands with plain objects,
Key, door handle, steering wheel,
But my hands are nothing:
A song you can't remember
The words to,
The button that pops
Off a vest, a comb that
Falls out of a pocket
Or purse.

Susan fills my lungs with air,
But what do I breathe out?
Parchment, ink, low growls, the
Blank gap between words.

Nothing fits upon my back,
Nothing actually catches my eye,
I am hidden and found,
I am North, South, East, West,
My dark skin porous, in-between.

Susan claims my name is muscle,
Bone, calls me tissue
And sinew, fills in my blank
With the absence of her boys,

But I am water, pebble,
Silt and gravity,
Evidence under her nail.

WHAT THE SHERIFF SUSPECTS

Each time the town tells the sheriff
To look harder, my nose straightens and
My hair uncurls. I rustle like wind upon
The surface of a lake. I wink just
Below Susan's cheeks.

The sheriff has shuffled my deck all week.
So many miles, so many deeds.
I do not tire. I can't stop driving. I can
Wrangle kids in broad daylight and never
Be seen or heard. I'm not doing this for ransom.
When I'm about, things simply don't add up,

A short distance becomes too large, clocks run amok,
Stop signs change into traffic lights. Now he wonders
Why he's never noticed the way Susan's body can't sit still,
My accent rising from her alibi.

NEXT OF KIN

The black man in town
They thought looked like me,
Without the dreamed-up cap
And wardrobe,

The police have him now.
He sits in a small room.
They turn him this way
And that.

He'll cool there for hours.
How do you think he feels?
I whisper *we're innocent*
Into his ears.

He looks so much like me,
We could be brothers.
Already, folks
May have their doubts:

He's poor enough.
Where has he been?
He has his needs.
What do they know?

Neighbors call him *quiet,*
A new knot of stress
On the tongue.

It's been a hard week
To be black in Union, S.C.,
A black woman tells a reporter,

The whites aren't civil.
They look at you and then
Reach over and lock
Their doors.

Now he is it.
Susan has lent me
His cheekbones,
His gait.

For a while,
He is as close as
They'll ever get.

WHAT IS KNOWN ABOUT THE ABDUCTOR

The sheriff reads off a list of things I have not done:
I have not called on the phone. I did not discard the
Childrens' clothing they found by the highway,

I wasn't the man who robbed a convenience store
In a car the same color as Susan's. I didn't drop
Off the child they found, in Seattle, in a child's
Seat like hers; the baby someone thought they
Heard crying in the woods; not there, none of
My doing.

Bloodhounds cannot catch a whiff of me. Divers
Rake the bottom of John D. Long Lake. I give
Them a snootful of silt. Who am I? Nothing
Says the sheriff, can be ruled out. A teenaged girl
Sees a man, covered in mud, walk out of the woods.

The heat sensors of the helicopter they send fail
To light my soggy footprints. Nothing can be
Dismissed. A psychic tumbles through a dream.
He nods as the children point everywhere but
In my direction. I am zip, my
Face and reasons an educated guess.
All week the police computers grind,

But I am that number after the decimal that keeps
Stuttering, won't resolve.

INTERROGATION

The children were fussy,
Susan tells the FBI agent,
So we strapped them in the back seat
And drove off to go shopping
At Kmart.

How can a black man drive
An old, beat-up Mazda
In a southern town
With two white kids
In the backseat,
And never be seen?
The agent would like an
Explanation.

He binds our arm to the
Polygraph,

But we swear we were in the
Parking lot,
In the hours before
I officially arrive,
Under the brute light
Of the mercury lamps.

Who could have missed us, diving
To find a bottle, wedged
Under the back seat?

Who didn't notice us
As we walked the aisles,
A cranky family among
The other cranky families?

He insists: what we say
Is not what we mean.
He tries to spike our heart.

We say, as evenly as we can: the children
Were twitchy bombs
Of sugar; first
We exhaust their eyes, then
Cruise the town,
Like any family,
Bargaining for sleep.

MY EYES

Susan hopes the sheriff will recognize what she's stitched
Under my lids. Perhaps I'm a young boy whose dark skin
Ricocheted off her and her friends on a playground.

Now I drive about, my gaze a blown switch. Maybe I'm
The first time she noticed where they say I'm fit to live: the
Wrong side of the tracks, chocolate town, coonville.

Haven't you seen those eyes before? she asks him, that ache
So close to yearning, the heart's fallen architecture as you see
How this world really works, the empty stare that tracks off
The map, somewhere beyond negotiation.

WHAT ISN'T KNOWN ABOUT THE ABDUCTOR

No name, no known jobs or affiliations.
Was I working alone, was someone else
Waiting to help? Did I intend to rob, carjack,
Or kidnap?

Why won't I stop? Am I afraid, do I think things
Have spun beyond my control? Why won't I
Simply drop the kids off somewhere?

Was I paid to do this? Did Susan promise me
Reward for taking her children?
Did I do anything sexual to her?

Why did I go for that particular car?
What sort of carjacker
Lies in wait on a deserted road?

No age, no preference, no known associates.
How long have I lived? Will I strike again?
Did I grab hold of a random opportunity?

Am I someone who lives in town?
How can I keep moving yet never be seen?
Why us?

PRESS CONFERENCE

And this is my life now.
I am a faint hum behind
The sensation, the blur of doubt
At the corner of the flashbulb.

These are my names these days:
Hungry, senseless, man of little
Schooling, ninny, fraidy-cat.

If I had an opinion, I guess
I would tell you all I'm tired,
Days and days of near misses,
Almost snapping into focus,

The in-between feel of circling
These streets, a rumor.
If I could, I'd let our weariness
Bite into the sheriff's ear.

Susan steps to the mike.
How do we feel?
There's a crack in our voice.

SYMPATHY

The sheriff's too good to be true.
He tries to urge Susan and me to part.
He trusts a friendly cup of coffee will skim me loose,
But we're hard to untangle.
I won't be easy; we know his help
Is poison. He is courting us.
We run a cold sweat
While he waits.
He is too good to be true.
I am not for his ears, Susan knows.
She tries not to weep; he attempts to lean toward us,
We bob together in the god-awful silence.

CONFESSION

There have been days I've almost
Spilled

From her, nearly taken a breath.
Yanked

Myself clean. I've
Trembled

Her coffee cup. I well
Under

Her eyelids. I've been
Gravel

On her mattress. I am
Not

Gone. I am going to
Worm

My way out. I have
Not

Disappeared. I half
Slide

Between her teeth,
Double

Her over as she tries
Not

To blurt me out. The
Closer

Susan inches me
Toward

This, the
Louder

The sheriff
Hears

Me bitch.

*The italicized language
is from Susan Smith's
handwritten confession.*

BIRTHING

*When I left my home on Tuesday, October 25, I
was very emotionally distraught*

I have yet
To breathe.

I am in the back of her mind,
Not even a notion.

A scrap of cloth, the way
A man lopes down a street.

Later, a black woman will say:
"We knew exactly who she was describing."

At this point, I have no language,
No tongue, no mouth.

I am not me, yet.
I am just an understanding.

▬

*As I rode and rode and rode, I felt
Even more anxiety.*

Susan parks on a bridge,
And stares over the rail.
Below her feet, a dark blanket of river
She wants to pull over herself,
Children and all.

I am not the call of the current.

She is heartbroken.
She gazes down,
And imagines heaven.

━━━━━

*I felt I couldn't be a good mom anymore, but I didn't want
my children to grow up without a mom.*

I am not me, yet.
At the bridge,
One of Susan's kids cries,
So she drives to the lake,
To the boat dock.

I am not yet opportunity.

━━━━━

I had never felt so lonely
And so sad.

Who shall be a witness?
Bullfrogs, water fowl.

──────

When I was at John D. Long Lake
I had never felt so scared
And unsure.

I've yet to be called.
Who will notice?
Moths, dragonflies,
Field mice.

──────

I wanted to end my life so bad
And was in my car ready to
Go down that ramp into
The water

My hand isn't her hand
Panicked on the
Emergency brake.

And I did go part way,
But I stopped.

I am not Gravity,
The water lapping against
The gravel.

I went again and stopped.
I then got out of the car.

Susan stares at the sinking.
My muscles aren't her muscles,
Burned from pushing.
The lake has no appetite,
But it takes the car slowly,
Swallow by swallow, like a snake.

Why was I feeling this way?
Why was everything so bad
In my life?

Susan stares at the taillights
As they slide from here
To hidden.

———

I have no answers
To these questions.

She only has me,
After she removes our hands
From our ears.

THE RUNNING MAN POEMS:

What follows is a cycle of most of the poems that became the libretto to Diedre Murray's score for *Running Man,* a jazz opera that had its premiere at the HERE Performing Arts Space, New York City, in February 1999.

Running Man is a tale that concerns itself with family, race, and morality. The main setting is a town somewhere on the Virginia coast, between the 1930s and the 1950s. As the poems (but not the play) open, Running Man is already dead, and his sisters, who now live in a city in the north, have just received the news of his passing. Running Man will return as a grown man, a child (Tommy), and a ghost. The characters are: MOTHER, FATHER, MISS LOOK (younger sister), MAMIE (older sister), SEVEN (spirit/root woman), and RUNNING MAN. The language italicized before a title is an excerpt from the libretto. The speaker of the poem/song is in parentheses.

Seven:
It's been seven years since Running Man gone
Seven long years—where is he now?

WHEN HE LEFT (MISS LOOK)

The word got around:
If you wanted somebody to figure
Something out,
You called Tommy.

He was good with words.
He had a way of looking
Into the heart of an object.
He was on a first-name basis

With a bloom or a motor.
He'd unlock books
And tame the jargon,

Take the white man's
Arithmetic
And make it spit
Silver dollars.

When he left,
The birds and trees lost
Their Latin names,

Our world shrank back
To just a world.

HOLD THE LINE (MAMIE)

When the only telephone in this apartment house rings
Everyone listens hard for a tap to run up the radiator.
This is the way we get the news from home.

Somebody's calling Harlem.
St. Lucie, Chicago, Kingston, New Orleans,
A gunshot, gossip, a birth, a garnishee.
An uncle coming up, a sister passing through.

Somebody's calling Harlem.
A buddy running toward wherever
Ain't isn't. Wire me down some cash.
So-and-so did such-and-such.

Somebody's calling Harlem.
Cancer, the sugar, the Lord Jesus, the law.
Fort Worth, Texas; Brazil, Indiana;
Gary, Oklahoma; Springfield, Tennessee.

Can't go no further but still can't go.
The weather, the weddings,
The white folks, the farm soil that
Clings to your city clothes.

Come home said the bullet that
Caught my brother, a two–one–two
Beat on the pipes. My grief rises off
The Chesapeake. He ghosts the Virginia clay,

The cradle of the phone,
My ear.

THE TRAIN (MISS LOOK)

This train we ride
Sixteen coaches long.
This train we ride
Sixteen coaches long.
You can ride all day
But never as long
As he'll be gone.

Our downstairs neighbor caught me
As I walked upstairs after work, to tell me
My brother, "your boy," as she put it, was dead.
She added a word or two about Jesus, but by then
I was up the landing and through the door.
I found my sister

Weeping, so I knew it was true.

Train, train rolling
Down that track
Train, train, just a-rolling
Down that track
You can ride those rails forever,
It'll never bring him back.

We got to go home
She said, back to Virginia to claim his body.
I heard the word *scandal,* I heard the word *murder,*
I saw two tickets in her hand. The long train, I thought,
We were going to ride misery through the night and

A good portion of the morning.

Jim Crow rules past
The Mason-Dixon Line.
Yeah, Jim Crow the boss
Below the
Mason-Dixon Line.
You can sup the engine cinders
If you care
To dine.

My sister already had our
Bags packed. I saw a cloud
Cross her face.

Train we ride
Home to the Chesapeake
Train we ride

Back home to the Chesapeake.
Gladly pay a million dollars
Just to hear my brother speak.

This, my neighbor yelled
After me, was the Lord's work,
His mysterious ways.

Mother:
Before he left for the war,
My man was so sweet.
Before he changed
From a husband to a soldier
That man was kind.

What did the Army send home?

When he looks at our boy, what does he see?

PISS (FATHER)

We black boys asked
This country
For a gun.

They give us
A shovel.

We defended our
Country
By digging
Privies.

They found
Barracks
Too tough

For a dog
Or a rat
To live in,

And handed us
The keys.

One afternoon
A white officer
Pulled down
His fly,
He laughed
As we dug,

He laughed
As he rained
Down
On us
Black boys,
Our backs
Stained

Defendin'
Freedom.

Before the war,
I used to think
A black man
With enough
Smarts
And backbone

Could win a place
In this world.

No more.

Seven (spoken to Miss Look):
You always thought it was his black bottom friends
That helped drag Tommy down.

But the truth, you see,
Came from his family!

ARMOR (MOTHER)

Some folks worry our people
But they're not going to worry
My boy.
Some folks listen in on our
Dreams,
Then grab a broom
And sweep them away.

But I'm going to make him strong
Like a river that wears away
A stone.
I'm going to make his mind
Fast as mercury.
You can't touch the sun
If you never reach.
The lessons I teach will be
Armor for his
Beauty.

Some folks tell our people
Thinking for ourselves
Is a sin.
But that isn't the world
I'm building for him.
Some folks would rather see

Black folk with our hands out
And down on our knees.
But that will never be.

I'm going to make him strong
Like a river that wears away
A stone.
I'm going to make his mind
Fast as mercury.
You can't touch the sun
If you never reach.
The lessons I teach will be
Armor for his
Beauty.

Father:
Never seen
A black person read
Like this before,
Like a root
Tapping water.

MAMIE (RUNNING MAN)

"Hey man?" asks my beloved eldest sister,
The woman who loves my
Deep brown eyes and will always
Cut me slack, *"What's that you're reading?"*
We both know the answer don't matter.

We live in a town
Not even a bible can cure.
I am the one she points out to her friends
And jokes:
And the Good Lord say: "Let this boy's hands
Be quick, stay soft, let them
Pull a trigger before they pull a boss's
Load!"

To her,
I am a rose, a green fuse cut through January turf.
Barely three years old when, so the story goes,
My tongue cracked open a printed word.

To her,
I am proof that maybe not everything happens
The way they say it should. She laughs
And tells me to keep on reading.
Sounds like a woman's spell.

FAILURE (RUNNING MAN)

One day my mother pointed
Up at the sky.
I saw a sparrow being
Snatched up by a hawk.
Someday, she said,
You're going to grow up
To be just like him.

She was speaking of the hawk,
But I was thinking about the sparrow.
And it didn't matter
That I turned my eyes away
Before its bloody feathers
Could hit the ground.

One day, she promised,
The world's going to surrender
Everything to what my shadow
Demands,
But I didn't feel the hunger
That keeps his talons sharp.

I thought about the dark cloud
That dropped
Upon that poor sparrow's breast.
Then I felt her hand fall lightly
On my shoulder.

Miss Look:
Are you there?
Are you real?
Am I dreaming?
Is it really your voice?
Is it only the breeze?

Are you here?
Are you cold?
Are you staying?
After so long, Tommy,
There's no gray in your
Hair.

HOME (RUNNING MAN)

You can walk from one end
To the other of my town
In a few heartbeats.

I guess it isn't even fair
To call it that.
It's Old Nancock, Virginia
On the Chesapeake,

Four or five buildings
Holding together
A dirt road.

Here are some things
The white folks
Let us keep:

A post office.
A general store.
A church.
A cemetery.

At night the old slaves
Dust themselves off
And rise from their
Graves

To catch a peek
Of the world
They never had.

They drift back
To the old shacks
We left standing,

Or to that place
In the swamp
Where their good luck
Turned hard.

From a speeding car
I'm sure it don't look
Like much:

Saw grass.
Seaweed.
Crickets.
Gull shit.
Everything you see
Says *keep going.*

There have always been
A few things
White folks
Won't bother with.

They drive by
And think of
Short ends
Of sticks.

To this day

You can still find
Chains
In the shacks.
It is a game we play
With our ghosts:

Their wrists
Are our wrists,
Our wrists
Are theirs,

And what's become
Of the key?

Miss Look:
The best part of my brother
Is the best part of my heart.

MISS LOOK'S DREAM (MISS LOOK)

Can I offer a bit of advice?
I am walking with my dead brother
I am dreaming on a train
We are in our favorite place, the slave cemetery,
The soil springs to our step and moss itches our nose,

This is our quiet. Africa lies under our feet.
I know this not from the school, but from
My brother, who forms the word in his mouth
Like the pastor says *God*, or the cracker says *Nigger*:
Like he owns it. All the flowers in this plot feed

On the dust of kings, princes, queens, he says.
And he laughs. One part honey, one part curse,
One part train whistle steaming through a crossing.
I nod my head in agreement to his features,
The clever music he speaks.

How can a head hold so much, I worry.
He has given me the names of things
And in my Sunday-school heart, I picture Adam
Painting the peacocks' feathers for his bride.
Go see the world, he suggests,

I am rolling back through it now, half-aware, clacking
These heavy miles home. The gulls caw
And clang in my mind. We sing our ancestors,
The clay under our rocking feet. The birth
Of coal, he tells me, is death,

A film of soot that cracks open my eyes.

BABY SISTER & THE RADIO (RUNNING MAN)

I am telling my baby sister how the radio works,
How, on a clear night, Nashville, Memphis &
Chicago are able to twang shout and holler at us.
I tell her what *broadcast* means: a hand tossing riffs
From a sack.

So the world is a big adventure, she thinks.
I bring to her attention olives and
Roman columns. I bring her Charlemagne
And Louis Armstrong.

She is restless, our Huck, half-full. It's like riding a
Secret highway out, I say,
And we tune in the evening stars.

MY SISTER MAKES ME UP WHILE I SLEEP
(RUNNING MAN)

I am pretty, but my sister knows
You can't have too much of a good thing.
She kisses my cheeks with rouge
And highlights the good things about
A black boy's face.

I am pretty, and she has watched as I enter
Our mother's closet, her treasure chest.
How soft, this type of swimming,
Pushing the slips and brushing
The various codes of fabrics.

I am pretty, and while sleeping, I am
Dolled Up. She buffs my high cheekbones
Into wings. She smears my
Innocent lips red with love.

Miss Look:
*I was too young
To know better.*

FIRST CRIMES (RUNNING MAN)

Nothing can run when you've broken its legs.
Nothing can fly when you trim its feathers
With a knife, a stone.

A fish, scooped from a pond
Flops like a dipsomaniac
Or a sinner, smacked to the floor

By the holy spirit! He reels and shakes
Himself free of what he'd been.

A beetle's shell
Cannot deny a pin.
A butterfly's wing

Is impossible!
A speck of parchment
And veins,

Tougher than
A breeze.

No matter how bright
Their husk, how fleet
Their limbs, how cunning
Their armor,

In the end
You can find their
Helplessness.

See their eyes
As they snap and tear
Apart,

Don't you think
They long to go back
To what they'd been:

A water breather,
A skimmer of air,
A fast shadow
Through tall grass?

I read in a book
We're all like this.

Sea water,
Breathing minerals,
Low sparks that sing.

Wouldn't you call that a miracle?

LIAR (RUNNING MAN)

My folded hands.
My gentle eyes.
The way my mouth gives
Nothing away.

Mothers detect
Hope in the way
I carry myself.

I am young
And they think

Maybe I'll escape
Becoming a certain type
Of man,

Whiskey-triggered,
Short-fused,
Go-up-side-the head
Paycheck burner.

And what do
The elders see?
I can read the white
Man's voodoo,

Powerful spells
Which have eaten
The world,

And prevented
Anything good
From sticking here.

I am young
And they hope

I will hone my studies
Into a terrible blade.

They think I'm good
And pat my strange head,
But no one's been
Properly introduced

To a boy who
Looks like me
But rumbles through
Small deaths,

Guts
On fence posts,
Bugs
On pins,

No one has tasted
My lips.
They've smacked
Blood and pin feathers.

My winning smile.
My confidence.
The sincere way
I look a man
In the eye.

Low expectation
Fattens me,
Sasses me up.

Who
Will catch me out?

I am young.
The town whispers
Maybe and *might*
Behind my back

Nobody knows
What I keep behind
My eyes.

Miss Look:
Don't you remember, daddy?
The way you treated him as a kid?

SEX (RUNNING MAN)

Then I start dreaming of him again,
But I know I'm not supposed to do this,
Even if his flesh is made of the finest honey
And his hair scents my nose.

I am still too young to know what to make
Of this. I yawn, and then off I drift
(And I have drifted to others)
And I am filled with his high laugh.

We are alone here, but I have been punished
For telling this out loud.
And I don't know why I should be hurt.
The way he laughs tickles my heart.

I nap, and he is the first thing I see.
It is like waking to the finest dinner on earth.
I don't want to hear my father and mother
Call me a fool, call me worse than a fool.

Every time I say this out loud I must feel pain.
This, they say, will make me stop. My father takes me
To the bathroom, he removes my pants
He takes a toothbrush and this pain he gives

Is approved of by Jesus. I bleed. It hurts to shit.
This will shut my mind, they hope,
But when the throbbing stops, and soon after my head
Hits the pillow, I am walking with him,

My friend, my beautiful boy, my dreamer,
Who doesn't know what I am learning.

REVENGE (RUNNING MAN)

When she looked at me, I knew I would take
Her goodwill, her lust, and abuse her heart.
We were in church. She decided I looked polite.
She saw my folded hands, my Sears and Roebuck
Pinstripes. I heard the crinoline rustle in her dress.

She was decent, and decided I was ready,
And I could tell everyone within eyesight was
Starting to agree: my relieved parents,
The parishioners nodding their countrified heads.
Before the last hymn shook the floorboards

I knew I would have to take her someplace quiet
And candle false hope. She stepped up to me
The way a puppy might,
Mistaking my scent for somebody kind. I took
Her hand. I saw duty in her hips.

I had abandonment to teach, cold sheets
To share, the tooth and claw of lies as
They hit in the bottom of the night.
She decided life had come to snatch her up.
She believed she gazed upon the face of better luck,

But I was careless love, an angel of revenge,
The swell of flood that paws away a random car
For the misfortune of crossing its path.

Running Man (to younger self):
One day he'll pay!
One day I'll get stronger
Someday he'll be older
He'll think I've forgotten
But I won't.

WHAT I DO (RUNNING MAN)

Why do what I do?
Sometimes for money,
Sometimes for kicks,

Sometimes to see the sweat
On the victim's brow.
Sometimes I believe I can
Smell their fear.

Sometimes it's hunger.
Sometimes it's like watching
Water flow over a stone.

Sometimes it's knowing
They'll wake up in a sweat
And wonder if I'll return.

Sometimes, it's weakness.
The flesh wants
What it wants,
My knuckles against
A cheek.

My fingers rifling
Through easy cash.
Sometimes it's because

They run,
And I know
I'm faster,

Or they try to
Fight back,
But I know I'm
Stronger,

Or they tried to hide it
But I know the angles
Before they think
Of the angles.

I am the running man.
The shadow in the corner
Of your eye,

The reason a grove of trees
Turns sinister in the dark.
Why not
Is my blood,
My story,
My middle name.

Mother:
Look at this man
My countrified man.
His ways are rough
As bark on the trees.

REPLACED (FATHER)

I should have seen the end at the beginning.
I should have seen it coming right from the start.
She dressed him up, cooed in his ears,
Sat my boy down at the head of the table.
She never needed a man. She longed for a companion,
A boyfriend as witty and high-class as herself.

I should have seen it right at the beginning.
He was her mirror. I was old hat.
I'd done my duty. That was that.
One day I came home, and my son was
The man of the house.
She never needed me. She longed for company
That was well-read and could hum symphonies.

I should have seen the end at the beginning.
I should have tasted her poison right from the start.
She had to pretend that she birthed an angel.
One day I came home, and my son was
Sitting at the top of the world.
I curse the curse the world's put on my skin.
I curse the curse she's put on him.

TRUTH (RUNNING MAN)

Then she says, "Don't hurt me!"
But this is after she says
She knows all my business,
And what's gonna happen to me
After she tells the world,

And you really have to wonder
What was in her mind
To tell me all this,
Like this was now going to
Stop me
From being me.

I mean,
She's laughing at me
After telling me
That I'm a crook
And a hustler,
And she knows I've killed
For far less than this.

Like this was going to stop my razor
From being my razor.
Then she looks me in the eye.

What did she expect?
First her eyes smirk,
Then they panic.

Then she looks at me
Like she's finally looking at me
For the first time.

WHAT HAPPENED (RUNNING MAN)

Everyone in town's
Swagging their finger,
Clucking behind my back.
Haven't seen Dollie
In a while,
She go visit her people?
And they smile like I ought
To drop to my black knees
And beg the Lord Jesus to forgive me.

But you know what?
I will walk up and down
The neighborhood,
I will look these so-called
Solid citizens
In their countrified eyes,
I will sing them the blues:

I once loved a gal,
But she found another,
I tried to hold on
But I just couldn't
Please her.

I'll give them
The details:

My emptied purse,
A train ticket,
A high-yellow boy
From Richmond,

And they'll think
Of their own
Back doors.
The rhythm
High-heels make
After a woman sets
Her mind.

If you think about it
Real careful,
It isn't like I'm telling
A full lie,

The woman did drive me
To distraction,
There really was a moment
I couldn't tell
Up from down,

For awhile
I was bedeviled.

When I buried her,
I howled like
A wolf had caught me
In its jaws.

There are mud
And pine needles
On the soles of
My boots,

A confession
Ground into
My work clothes.

I'm the running man.
A good-timer,
A hi-stepper.
As long as I supply,
I'm allowed.

If I say my baby hopped
A train,
You can bet
That train has smoked
And gone.

I can lie.
They can kiss my ass.

GOSSIP/DENIAL (TOWN/MOTHER)

(That boy ain't right!
He ain't never been right!
That's what we heard!
That's what we know!)

There's a picture in the paper
Of my son,

(His mama don't know
How he makes his dough!
No she don't!)

On Main Street
In a Coupe de Ville.
The top is down.

(When he ain't beating
Somebody down
In a back alley,
He's shootin' up!
He's a crook!)

If the white folk
Have a problem with
The black folk,
He's the man they call.

(She never hear him say
'Your money, or your life'!)

There's a picture in the paper
Of my boy.

(The cons can't con him,
And the law—they scared of him!)

Look at his suit,
It is silk and powder-blue.

(Who does he think he is
Learning all that stuff?
He thinks he's better than
Everyone else!)

It cost big money,
He gives it all away.

(What did all that learnin' do?
Just a waste!
Cocaine!
Heroin!
I hear he rents a cot
At the barrelhouse!
Walking around
Like a circus freak!)

There's a picture of my son
In the middle of Main Street,

(Her 'special angel'!
He ain't nothin' but a
Cigarette pimp!)

In a Caddy
In a Coupe de Ville.
The top is down.

(Who does she think
She's foolin'!
Lord help her if she
Ever finds out!)

If a poor neighbor dies
My son foots the bill.
I gaze long and long
At my boy.

Seven:
What made that poor boy go bad?
Changed sweet honey
To strychnine?

HUNGER (RUNNING MAN)

You don't know
How hunger feels,
How it salts your blood.

You've never felt a kiss
So deep
You want to die
Just so it can bring you back
To life.

You don't know
What it's like.
I was nothing.

You've never felt fear
Gnaw into you.
No idea
What hunger
Can do.
Crawling is the way
This snake sheds its skin.

DENOUNCEMENT (MISS LOOK)

How far you think
I'd go?
How long you think
I'd carry you?

You stole.
You dealt.
Each time I tried to help,
You slapped my hand away.

A bird can't live
With a snake.
I had to let you go.

How often did you think
I'd turn a blind eye?
How many times
Could you go to
The well?

You catted.
You lied.
You beat down your
Mama.

A snake can't live
With an eagle.
I had to throw you out.

You want me to feel
Regret.
There's no tears in
My eyes.

A fox can't live
With a hare.
I had to show you
My back.

Family:
I wonder why
This life has so much misery

RUNNING MAN

I am the running man.
The shadow in the corner
Of your eye,

The reason a grove of trees
Turns sinister in the dark.

Why not
Is my blood,
My story,
My middle name.

God made me pretty.
God made me smart.
God made me black,
Which only proves

God's infinite sense of humor.

Where I come from,
A smart black boy
Is like being a cat
With a duck's bill.

Where I live
The neighbors say
He's so bright
But mean
He's so white

And stare in awe
And pity as
I keep turning
Pages.

Call me a
Useless miracle.

Until my eyes
Fell upon the
Page,
I was just
A drowsy boy.

I admit the words
Tickled my ear
And shook
My tongue
My teeth,

I'm sure it looked
Like violation.

I'm sure it looked like
Anger, slowly
Rinsing over
My body.

I was talking
In another tongue,
The language
That measured
Me and mine
Less,

The civilized tones
Which burned
And noosed
And dusted our roofs
With never enough.

Perhaps my folks withdrew
From the sight
Of me, eyes
Thrilled

As the words
Chose me.

I am the running man.
The chill you feel
Blowing out
A back alley.

When you say *no*
But mean *yes*
You have passed
My doorstep.

I am whispered.
I rise on anger's
Updrafts.

Where in the world
Will he land,
Worried my folks,
This pretty black
Hatchling?
What pushes him up

Will keep him down.

ABOUT THE AUTHOR

Formerly director of the Poetry Center at SUNY/Stony Brook, CORNELIUS EADY is currently Distinguished Writer-in-Residence at the City College of New York. His many awards include the Academy of American Poets Lamont Prize, a Rockefeller Foundation Fellowship to Ballagio, and fellowships from the Lila Wallace Reader's Digest Foundation, the John Simon Guggenheim Foundation, and the National Endowment for the Arts. Widely anthologized, Eady is the author of six volumes of poetry, including *Victims of the Latest Dance Craze, You Don't Miss Your Water,* and *The Autobiography of a Jukebox.* With poet Toi Derricotte, he co-founded Cave Canem, which offers workshops and retreats for African-American poets, and with composer Diedre Murray, he has collaborated on two highly acclaimed music-dramas, *You Don't Miss Your Water* and *Running Man.*